THE NESS OF BRODGAR

ORKNEY

Stones of Stenness

c **3600-3300** BC
settlements at
Knap of Howar;
Braes of Ha'breck,
Wyre; Smerquoy

c **3400-3100** BC
Earliest
structures built
at the Barnhouse
settlement, 300
metres from the
Ness across the
Loch of Harray

Barnhouse

c **3000** BC
Tomb of the
Eagles, South
Ronaldsay;
early buildings
at Skara Brae,
six miles to NW
of the Ness of
Brodgar

THE NESS

Fifteen generations separate the early
settlers on the Orkney archipelago from the
architects of the Ness of Brodgar – an island
centre that would endure for 60 generations.
The last occupants left the Ness 4000 years
ago and for 200 generations it has lain,
forgotten, beneath the plough.

c **3300-3200** BC
Earliest
structures built
at the Ness of
Brodgar. These
have not yet
been reached by
the excavators

c **3100** BC
Series
of oval
buildings
and
enclosure
walls built

View from the Ness

BRITAIN AND IRELAND

c **3900** BC **Flint
mines and stone
axe quarries; first
long barrows and
chambered tombs;
Balbridie timber
hall, Aberdeenshire**

c **3700** BC
**Causewayed
enclosures;
Cleaven Dyke
Cursus, Perth
and Kinross**

c **3500** BC **Cursus
monuments in
Southern Britain**

c **3300** BC
**Newgrange
under
construction
in the Boyne
Valley, Ireland**

c **3100** BC
**Phase 1
enclosure a
Stoneheng
Cairnpapp
Hill Henge
West Lothi**

THE NESS THROUGH TIME

3000 BC 2800 BC 2600 BC 2400 BC 2200 BC

c **3000-2900** BC
Standing Stones
of Stenness built

c **3000-2500** BC
Settlement at
Links of Noltland,
Westray

c **2900-2750** BC
Barnhouse
settlement
abandoned

c **2700** BC
Construction
of Maeshowe
chambered
cairn

c **2600-2500** BC
Ring of Brodgar
built

c **2450** BC
Skara Brae
abandoned

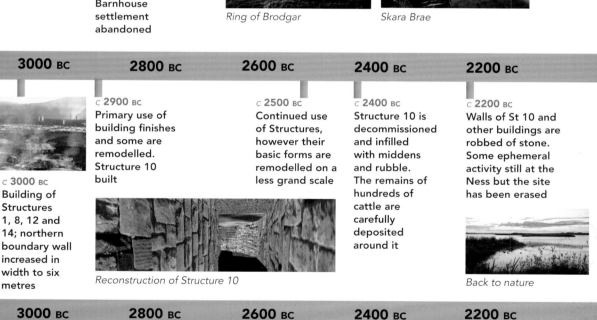

Ring of Brodgar

Skara Brae

3000 BC 2800 BC 2600 BC 2400 BC 2200 BC

c **3000** BC
Building of
Structures
1, 8, 12 and
14; northern
boundary wall
increased in
width to six
metres

c **2900** BC
Primary use of
building finishes
and some are
remodelled.
Structure 10
built

c **2500** BC
Continued use
of Structures,
however their
basic forms are
remodelled on a
less grand scale

c **2400** BC
Structure 10 is
decommissioned
and infilled
with middens
and rubble.
The remains of
hundreds of
cattle are
carefully
deposited
around it

c **2200** BC
Walls of St 10 and
other buildings are
robbed of stone.
Some ephemeral
activity still at the
Ness but the site
has been erased

Reconstruction of Structure 10

Back to nature

3000 BC 2800 BC 2600 BC 2400 BC 2200 BC

c **3000-2800**-BC
Thornborough
Henges,
Yorkshire

c **2900** BC
Callanish stone
circles, Lewis;
Avebury Henge,
Wiltshire

c **2800** BC
Great stone circles
and henges in
Cumbria

c **2500** BC Major stone
settings at Stonehenge
and Avebury; Durrington
Walls Henge/settlement;
Silbury Hill under
construction

c **2300** BC
Round barrows;
metalwork starts
to be made and
distributed

WHAT IS THE NESS OF BRODGAR?

This elegant finger of land, flanked by two lochs and encircled by some of Orkney's finest archaeological sites, has revealed itself to be one of the glories of the European Neolithic; the very centre of an ancient world.

The Neolithic structures at the Ness of Brodgar are unique. There is nothing quite like them in the Neolithic of Atlantic Europe. They were in use for at least a millennium, and perhaps a good deal longer than that. Dating and theories about this remarkable site are reviewed and refined constantly, and are themselves frequently overturned by new discoveries.

The European Neolithic is a period which began in Britain around 4000 BC and came to an end at the Ness around 2300 BC. The best evidence so far is that building began at the Ness around 3300 BC with Structure 1 built around 3000 BC, the magnificent Structure 10 constructed around

▼ **LOOKING ACROSS THE SITE** with Structure 14 in the foreground, Structure 8 beyond and Structure 10 top left. Just beyond is the house of *Lochview* with labs and office facilities.

2900 BC and still in use 600 years later. Older buildings lie beneath those currently exposed by our excavations.

The significance of the site is becoming clearer each year. The size, quantity and quality of the buildings, and the rich assemblages of artefacts found in and around them, suggest that the site was not simply domestic. The Ness is built in a central position in the Orkney archipelago and in the middle of its most imposing complex of monuments. This was a place of pivotal importance to the Neolithic people who lived in the more modest settlements that we find scattered across Orkney. It was the heart of their world.

This was a place of meeting, of coming together for people from all over Orkney and likely from further afield. Why? For feasting, trading, gossiping, performing rituals and above all else, for celebrating the important political and celestial events that defined the complex and vibrant society of the time.

▲ **A REDISCOVERED WORLD (left to right)** Two beautiful polished stone tools; Jo with her prize find; Grooved Ware pottery with decoration; Mick excavating yet more pottery; a pecked orthostat (upright stone) in Structure 10.

▶ **A PLAN OF THE MAIN STRUCTURES** At the right of the plan is the very large Structure 10 with its back wall penetrating Structure 8. Bottom left is Structure 12, with Structure 1 above it and to the left, and Structure 14 at the top. Structure 7 lies between Structures 1 and 8. Further buildings underlie the current plan; some are just visible, others yet to be excavated.

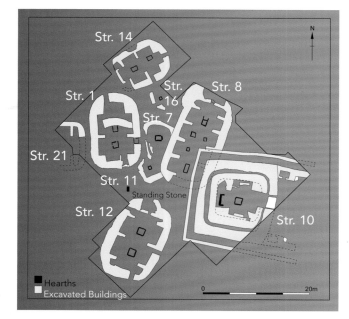

Str. 14
Str. 1
Str. 16
Str. 8
Str. 7
Str. 21
Str. 11
Standing Stone
Str. 12
Str. 10
■ Hearths
□ Excavated Buildings
0   20m

DISCOVERY AND EXCAVATION

A beautiful incised stone was found at the Ness in the 1920s, but it was not until 2003 that modern ploughing uncovered a large worked stone, setting in train the excavation that revealed this extraordinary site.

To see the Ness of Brodgar now you would never think that a decade or so ago it was a large, gentle grassy mound in an agricultural field. True, occasional prehistoric artefacts had been found on the surface before, but it took the plough to unearth a large stone slab which had clearly been fashioned in prehistory. It looked like the side slab of a Bronze Age burial cist, a stone coffin for the dead.

This implied the presence of human remains, which must be excavated with particular care and sensitivity. Exploratory work began, but what the excavators found was much more dramatic than an isolated burial. The tops of walls with superb stonework and crisp, zig-zag architectural lines emerged, instantly suggesting Neolithic buildings. It was our first glimpse of Structure 1, probably the

▼ GEOPHYSICAL SURVEY suggested there were walls beneath the ground surface; map with an early exploration trench; the stone slab that sparked the original excavation (the notched edge allows hands to lift it safely).

▲ **AN EARLY FIND**
A small fired clay
object with two
depressions,
perhaps for holding
coloured pigment.

oldest, and certainly one of the most impressive structures presently seen at the Ness.

That first glimpse was enough to warrant further investigation. Geophysics experts probed the ground, producing complex plans full of tantalising signals from beneath the surface. A dozen test pits were dug to verify the geophysics. All but one of them brought more evidence of handsome Neolithic walls into view, suggesting strongly that not only was this a Neolithic site, but one of remarkable size and complexity, containing some of the most magnificent structures yet found in Atlantic Scotland.

But what was it? Could it be a Neolithic settlement or something much more exciting in a location already famous for its monuments?

▲ **A TEAM OF STUDENTS** from all over the world uncover the walls of Structure 10 in 2008. Behind is the tool store and to the left, *Lochview* under which Structure 10 runs. No, we will not be knocking the house down.

WHAT IS MIDDEN?

When the structures at the Ness went out of use in prehistory they were covered over with rubble and many tonnes of midden. The word 'midden' implies rubbish or trash but the midden at the Ness turned out to be a gold mine, of huge importance for archaeologists and also, as it happens, for the people of the Neolithic.

The midden was, and is, full of artefacts such as pottery, stone tools and environmental evidence which provide vital glimpses into the lives of the people who deposited it. Analysis showed it also contained fertile, carefully manured agricultural soils which would have been of great value to Neolithic farmers. There is so much of it that it must have come from far and wide. And so, a place of great significance was eventually hidden under a blanket of precious soil, reinforcing archaeologists' belief that 'rubbish' is never just rubbish.

THE NESS IN THE LANDSCAPE

In 1999 UNESCO's World Heritage Committee granted a group of Orkney's Neolithic monuments World Heritage Status, naming them and their surroundings 'The Heart of Neolithic Orkney'. The complex at the Ness – discovered in 2003 – lies at the centre of that ancient landscape.

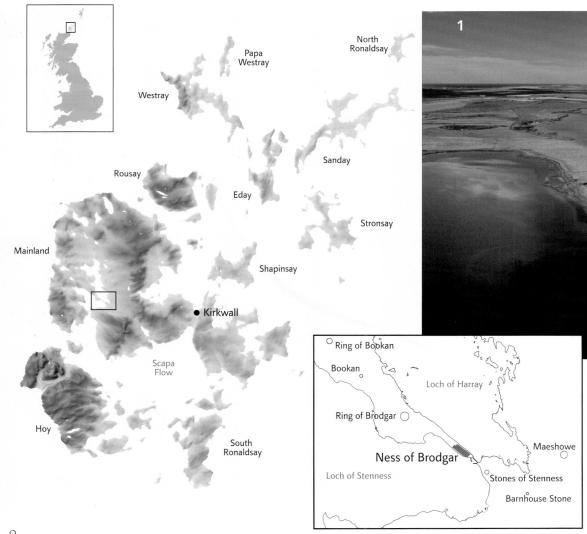

North Ronaldsay

Papa Westray

Westray

Rousay

Eday

Sanday

Stronsay

Mainland

Shapinsay

● Kirkwall

Scapa Flow

Hoy

South Ronaldsay

○ Ring of Bookan

Bookan ○

Loch of Harray

Ring of Brodgar ○

Ness of Brodgar

Maeshowe ○

Loch of Stenness

Stones of Stenness

Barnhouse Stone

WORLD HERITAGE SITE

1 the Ness of Brodgar with the Ring of Brodgar to the northwest and the Watchstone by the causeway to the southeast; 2 the Ring of Brodgar; 3 the Stones of Stenness; 4 Maeshowe; 5 the Watchstone and the Ness. Skara Brae, also part of the World Heritage Site, lies to the northwest on the Atlantic coast.

TWO LOCHS

The freshwater Loch of Harray is the largest on Mainland Orkney. The Loch of Stenness to the south is a sea loch flowing out to the Bay of Ireland and the Hoy Sound. The loch and its surrounding area underwent geophysical and sonar surveys in 2011-12 to investigate the drowned landscape. Results suggest archaeological features lie beneath the waters.

MONUMENTAL BUILDINGS

Many archaeologists spend entire careers excavating stains in the ground, perhaps left by rotted wood, bodies or rubbish pits. Not so the archaeologists of the Ness, who have the incredible good fortune to be uncovering standing buildings made of worked stone.

Everyone comes to the Ness for the first time with preconceptions. Perhaps they have seen it on television or in a magazine, but the first glimpse of these huge buildings, looking almost as they were left four thousand and more years ago, is a jaw-dropping moment. To say they are impressive is an understatement, for to see them is to imagine what it would be like to walk through their doors, to sit down and warm yourself at the hearths and perhaps stir a pot on the fire.

These walls also hide the secrets of how they were built. Careful examination shows complicated construction techniques and, just as important, evidence for remodelling and repair over time, sometimes out of dire necessity.

▲ **PASSAGE PAVING** The only way to understand these monumental structures is to excavate and record them. That is what is taking place here in the passage between Structure 10 and Structure 26.

STONE TILED ROOFS

This picture shows jumbled flagstones lying in Structure 8. At first glance they looked like material for a flagstone floor. Closer inspection showed they were far too thin for that purpose: they would have broken if stood upon. Further examination revealed trimming and shaping round the edges, together with traces of clay. What were they? The answer is truly extraordinary; they are our first evidence for the Neolithic use of stone as roof tiles. Most of the structures have them and they lie where they fell when the roofs collapsed, thousands of years ago.

None of this would have been possible without the extraordinary stone of Orkney, the flagstone found all over the islands, on the beaches and in the many small quarries which still pepper the landscape. Flagstone splits easily in the horizontal plane and is simple to trim – if you know what you're doing, that is. A humble product, it can be finely worked and skilfully laid, course upon course, to make the arrow-straight walls, internal partitions and furniture that make up these monumental structures.

It is the presence and workability of this stone, so much more durable than wood, which is the reason the Ness is still with us, and so imposing, while wood and turf structures of more recent times have decayed and disappeared.

▶ MAGNIFICENT COMPLEXITY
Sometimes you just have to stop and think. Site director Nick (and his favourite hat) contemplate fresh complexities in one of the major structures at the Ness.

▲ MASTER CRAFTSMAN
Nobody has taken better pictures of the Ness than Jim Richardson, the legendary American photographer who has virtually lived on site for several summer excavations and who still visits regularly. Above is an example of Jim's remarkable art, carefully lit by his assistants on a luminous midsummer night. Structure 1 stands out proudly in the foreground.

PHENOMENAL POT

Pottery is one of the great survivors on archaeological sites. It is often broken but is rarely destroyed if buried. The Ness of Brodgar pottery is especially extraordinary and it pours from the site, some of it of types and technologies never seen before.

The bulk of the pottery found at the Ness is called Grooved Ware. Much of it is decorated, sometimes by incising with a sharp point or by applying strips of clay on the surface in patterns. It is found all over Britain, and early archaeologists believed that advances in society, like new pottery forms, probably originated in the south and spread northwards. They looked south to continental Europe but found nothing that resembled Grooved Ware. With the advent of radiocarbon dating in the 1950s pots could be dated by the material in and around them. To everyone's surprise, the oldest dates for Grooved Ware are from Orkney. It was first made here around 3100 BC and spread outwards, turning archaeological theories upside down.

◀ ▼ EMBELLISHED POTTERY
Applied decorated pot under excavation; below left: incised pottery; centre: impressed, where a point or cord is pressed into the clay; right: applied, where clay pellets are pressed onto the surface.

WHAT POT REVEALS

Pieces of pottery are full of information; the trick is to know how to analyse them. The tiny thumb pot on the left could have held colour pigment which, although not visible, may have soaked into the fabric. Chemical analysis will reveal it. Burnt material on the inside of pot can be dated and analysis of fats can reveal whether meat or dairy produce was processed in the vessels. The clay and other material within the pottery itself can be analysed to determine whether it was gathered locally to the site, as can identification of the remains of microscopic creatures in the fabric. All these techniques, and more, are in use at the Ness.

▲ COLOURED VESSELS A number of vessels at the Ness are coloured, often on or up to applied decoration and in black, white and red. The red is haematite (an iron oxide) the black is soot and the white is… a mystery.

◀ MASSIVE POT SPREAD Mick and Helen carefully excavate several large, squashed slabs of pottery, probably from a storage vessel.

MACE HEADS, AXES AND

The people of the Ness were fortunate in their natural environment which provided a vast range of raw materials for fashioning tools. Their ingenuity and their skill in making use of these resources is staggering.

hammerstones, and maceheads.

The investigation of the various rocks present at the Ness has become a vital new subject for study. It is becoming clear that the people who used the site were highly skilled at selecting rock that exactly suited their purpose. Flint could be worked or knapped into sharp cutting, scraping or drilling implements. Glaciers brought a good deal of flint to Orkney, which the people of the Ness made good use of. They also obtained flint from

▲ CARVED STONE BALLS are almost exclusive to Scotland and this is our first. Their purpose is a mystery, yet hold one in your hands and you simply have to turn it. Could that be a clue?

Foremost amongst those materials was rock. Beyond the quarried flagstone and sandstone used in the buildings, there were many others, such as flint, granite, gneiss, basalt and camptonite: materials that could be made into arrowheads, points and knives, axes,

▶ A CAREFULLY DEPOSITED STONE AXE
Stone tools have life stories of their own, which intertwine with those of their owners. Their condition, treatment and context give clues to those relationships.

CARVED STONE BALLS

further afield, some of it as raw material or as finished artefacts.

Other rocks, like granite, were made into hammerstones, grinders and pounders, while some, like camptonite or gneiss were fashioned into visually striking items such as maceheads and carved stone balls. Rocks were not just chosen for utility. The look of the finished tool mattered too, a balance of colour, contrast and lustre. How it felt in the hand was also important, a quality that applies to many of the artefacts at the Ness.

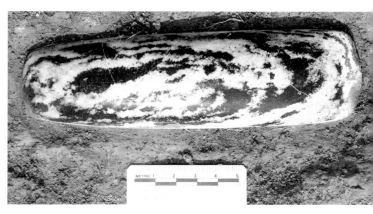

▲ **POLISHED AXE** This beautiful axe is like a summer sky with white, puffy clouds. Fashioned from gneiss it reminds us that, for some stone tools, looks really mattered.

◀ **CUSHION STONE** This shiny object is a cushion stone, used for grinding and polishing. It tells us that even simple grinding stones could be a labour of love.

▼ **MACEHEAD** This macehead has broken across the hole made for a wooden handle. Some seem to have been broken deliberately and buried formally, perhaps on the death of their owner.

◀ **CAREFUL RECOVERY** A plastic box and acid-free paper (to avoid contamination) represent a new form of burial for this cushion stone from Structure 8. Rarely for stone, it degraded after deposition due to acid soil conditions.

ART OF STONE

Decorated stonework has been recognised in Orkney at a number of tombs and settlement sites. None of this prepared the team at the Ness for the explosion of decorated stone discovered at the site.

All of the main structures have yielded examples of decorated stone; there are now well over 600 of them. The decoration is often lightly incised with a sharp implement, but there are also examples of deep carving, of pecking and of cup-marked decoration. There are portable decorated stones, but also examples of decoration on the walls of the structures, and even on stones within the walls or with the decoration facing wall interiors, as if hidden. Extraordinarily, some of the stonework in structures was also painted, particularly in Structures 1 and 8.

There are no simple explanations for this. The placing of the stone and its execution suggest that it was not simply decoration or casual 'doodling'. Instead there is a sense that creating decorated stone was a crucial part of the building and living process, intimately linked to the identity of its creators.

▶ **COLOSSAL LOAD** Beautiful as it is, this massive incised stone poses a threat to life and limb as it is lifted from the trench. Here, Andy and others grapple with it. Eventually it was lifted in a fishing net.

▼ THE BUTTERFLY STONE REJOINED
This magnificent decorated slab was discovered in three separate pieces, and they join! It is covered with 'butterfly' motifs which occur often at the Ness. The right-hand edge suggests other pieces may yet be found.

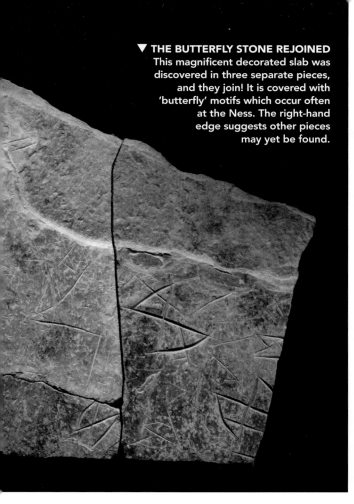

▲ RECORDING IN-SITU Part of the butterfly stone (pictured left) is photographed by Dave. Photography is a vital part of the recording of the site but incised stone, particularly if damaged or lightly worked, is difficult to capture.

▶ EXTRAORDINARY MARKINGS The multi-cupped stone and the cup-and-ring pecked stone (both grey) were found in Structure 10, the first in the entrance, the second amongst demolition deposits. The triangular stone is a handsome example of relief carving.

17

STRUCTURE 1
THE HEART OF THE NESS

This handsome structure is at least 5,000 years old, although it looks as if it was built yesterday. Its crisp, angular internal architecture is instantly recognisable and it lies at or near the very centre of the complex in its earliest days.

The first to be discovered, and maybe one of the first to be built, Structure 1 (see plan on page 5) is very similar to Building 2 at the Neolithic site of Barnhouse, just 300 metres to the southeast and easily visible from the Ness. Like nearby buildings it has an older structure underneath it but, unlike them, it has not slumped or subsided. What you seen now is Phase 2 of its complex history. Originally, it was much bigger, shaped inside like

▲ **STRUCTURE 1** from above. The hearth at the centre is clearly visible. To the left is the inserted wall of Phase 2. The grey line running diagonally across the left of the building is the water pipe that supplies the nearby farm.

▶ VIEWING THE SITE Structure 1 in the foreground; behind, the Loch of Harray and two site huts to left. The blue structure with people is the hugely popular viewing platform which allows great views of the site. It is funded annually by well-wishers.

a double cross and extending to the north for at least 15 metres.

The major changes which took place may be related to a change of function. Whatever the reason, it was shortened by the insertion of a large curved wall, two original doors were blocked and a new door was created to one side. Excavation over the past few years has shown that Structure 1 is one of the major repositories of stone artwork with numerous examples on the inside and outside of many of the walls.

The apparently central position of Structure 1 is enhanced by the slightly younger buildings which surround it and by the significant open space to the south, which it flanks and in many respects defines.

▼ A CLOSER LOOK (left to right) A view through the south entrance of Structure 1 to the central area with standing stone; excavation continues on the central area; an alcove in the walls containing a cache of stone tools.

STRUCTURES 8 AND 14
MULTIPLE PIERS AND PAINTED WALLS

These two structures represent the opposite ends of the size scale for piered structures, for Structure 8 is the largest and Structure 14 the smallest. Piers are the little stone walls which project into the interior of the structures, dividing it into separate spaces.

▶ **COLOURED WALLS** One of the first examples of coloured stone, forming part of the facing of a wall. Red, black and yellow colouring is clearly visible on the stone's edge.

Structure 8 was probably built just after Structure 1 and is one of the most remarkable buildings on site. It has five pairs of piers, 10 side recesses and six hearths. It has suffered catastrophic subsidence and has at least two earlier structures nestled underneath it. Finally it collapsed and was partly cleared for the construction of Structure 10.

Structure 8 is full of surprises. It was the first to reveal stone roof tiles and the first to display coloured pigment on the walls. It housed amazing artefacts, including a whalebone macehead, a whale's tooth in a stone setting and stone spatulas.

Structure 14 has a similar design to Structure 8 and, like Structure 1, is very

◀ ▼ **STRUCTURE 8** At the top of the picture a small, dark rectangular feature in the middle marks where the floor slumped, bringing down the roof and tiles. Traces of earlier buildings are visible under the pier to the right. Below are the roof tiles, stacked and ready for removal.

similar to Building 2 at Barnhouse. It has three entrances and two hearths, was constructed and reconstructed and ignominiously robbed of much of its stone in antiquity for reuse elsewhere. Its end sections seem to have been used for different purposes and chemical analysis of the floors should give us the details. Those floors hid fascinating artefacts including the magnificent blue and white stone axe on page 15.

▲ **STRUCTURE 14** from above. To the right of the picture is the area where robbers in antiquity took stone from the wall.

STONE SPATULAS

These beautiful artefacts, unique to the Ness, carefully worked from fine-grained rock and shaped and smoothed to perfection, were all found in Structure 8. Clearly they are tools, indeed one was found with other artefacts, perhaps constituting a tool kit, but we don't yet understand their purpose.

The two on the left are like long spoons but the 'bowl' end is flat and the outer edges are very delicate and have been fashioned with great care. It is possible they all might have been used in the smoothing of pottery but they don't show signs of wear and some may have been too fragile. All suggestions welcome.

STRUCTURE 10
400 HEAD OF CATTLE

It is known as the temple – a magnificent building with dressers, incised and painted stones, pigment, drains, a huge entrance and hundreds of deliberately deposited bones. What was this enigmatic building?

▲ **CATTLE AND DEER** Ingrid Mainland and her assistant excavate the bones found in the passageway around Structure 10.

▼ **ENTRANCE STONE** Mark Edmonds examines the entrance area. The huge stone is Structure 10's 'welcome mat'.

With Structure 10 we move up a gear, into what is acknowledged as some of the finest Neolithic architecture in Northern Europe. It is simply enormous: some 25 metres long, 19 metres across, with 4 metre thick walls and standing stones guarding its entrance. In the central hearth there was an upturned cattle skull; free-standing dressers line the walls. It has many examples of decorated stone and little dishes containing pigment point to a love of colour. This is not a run-of-the-mill domestic building. The masonry itself, each stone selected and laid with great skill, made a dramatic statement.

It was built around 2900 BC, remodelled due to structural instability perhaps a hundred years later, then used until around 2400 BC when something extraordinary happened. Perhaps as a ceremony to mark its 'decommissioning' a huge feast was held, hundreds of cattle were slaughtered and consumed, and some of their bones placed in the surrounding covered passageway, along with cattle skulls and complete deer carcasses. A monumental end to a monumental building.

▲ **NEOLITHIC ART** Decorated stone with incised triangles and small cup marks, found under a corner buttress which was used to reinforce the building when it became unstable. We can date the area to c2800 BC as the stone was found in association with an unusual Grooved Ware vessel containing carbonised, and thus dateable, material. The vessel also held a single bone from a new-born calf.

▼ **HAEMATITE** an iron oxide found in Orkney and used to create red pigment.

▲ FINE FURNITURE; UNUSUAL FINDS A dressed red sandstone pillar which was part of a dresser opposite the entrance of Structure 10. The dresser would have been a striking red and cream.

Nick and Mike examine a stone tool and here it is, revealed as a pestle macehead. It is unusual because it is unfinished. It should have a carefully drilled hole in the middle for a wooden handle.

STRUCTURE 12
MASTER BUILDERS

This fine building is both filled and surrounded with the crushed and broken remains of huge pottery vessels, while shaped and dimpled stone tools suggest that work took place here.

Structure 12 was beautiful when newly built. We know this because of the fine carved and dressed stone used in its construction. But it was built on poor foundations and required major renovation. Later builders, who added an annexe to the north, made a bad job of things. Piers are 'wonky', and walls are badly joined, making them more susceptible to slumping. Even so, the quality of the stonework shines through.

Structure 12 also contained examples of Grooved Ware pottery of a type not seen before. The annexe was full of pot, much of it coloured red, black and white. Just inside the northeast end more pottery was found, made with techniques that were not used again until Roman times.

▲ POT, TOOLS AND 'BUTTERFLY STONE' (left to right) A large sherd of pottery decorated with applied cordons (strips of clay applied to the surface) is ready to be photographed prior to lifting; the large stone is an anvil and one of many stone tools lies beside it in what is undoubtedly a working area; a beautifully incised 'butterfly stone' is uncovered – the motif was clearly an important one at the Ness.

▼ END VIEW Structure 12 looking towards the Loch of Harray.

◄◄ TRACES OF MAGNIFICENCE (far left) Tapered pier constructed of finely dressed stone but not keyed properly into the wall behind; (left) Structure 12 from above. The annexe which held masses of pottery is top right while at the bottom the wall has mostly disappeared due to later stone robbing. An entrance stood in the centre of the wall here and was flanked by two standing stones.

GREAT WALLS
AND GREAT MOUNDS

The complex at the Ness extends way beyond the main excavations. Enclosing walls and a mound to the south provide a tantalising hint of activity across the entire peninsula.

▲ **AERIAL VIEW** showing, in the field beyond the house, the scar of Trench T. The mound continues upslope to the left and downslope to the loch.

◄ **THE 'LESSER WALL'** with its beautifully regular stone work and vertical stance.

Many more structures at the Ness remain to be excavated. They extend in all directions, some even discovered on the far side of the road. In fact, the buildings you see now constitute less than 10 per cent of the total site. By good fortune, the structures already excavated may be the very heart of the site, as they are bounded by two massive walls. The walls were first spotted by geophysics, running across the peninsula from loch to loch. The 'Great Wall' of Brodgar, to the north, was 4 metres wide with an external ditch. It was then extended to 6 metres and is wider than Hadrian's Wall. The so-called 'Lesser Wall,' to the south, is 2 metres wide but constructed of beautiful stonework, still standing perfectly straight at 1.8 metres high, despite being built on an earlier structure. These are not defensive walls, but they define the structures and mark them out as special in relation to the buildings outside. They draw a line that clearly mattered to people back then.

Another surprising structure has been identified in Trench T, excavated outside the 'Lesser Wall' to the south. It is a huge, grassy mound and there were high hopes that it contained a chambered tomb. It is, instead, one of the largest heaps of midden ever discovered. It contains pottery, stone tools, standing stones, and buried near the top the skull of a very large cow or bull. This may be an aurochs, a wild ancestor of modern cattle. It all speaks of conspicuous consumption in the later Neolithic, a flow of food and other materials into the Ness that finds no parallels elsewhere in Orkney.

▶ TRENCH T
The section of the trench to the right has been excavated down into the midden. To the left are the stones and semi-circular structure which are part of an intrusion by Iron Age people around 2,000 years ago. It is common in Orkney to find that Iron Age folk utilised earlier structures and often remodelled them.

DID BRODGAR LOOK LIKE THIS?

This imaginative reconstruction by artist Aaron Watson gives a good impression of what the Ness may have looked like at its height. The stone roofs are prominent and strikingly similar to many old Orkney houses, while the people at the structure entrances remind us that they are the reason why the Ness and its wonderful artefacts exist.

We have the structures and the artefacts from the Ness and so we can say a good deal about them. We do not have the people, but their works can tell their story across time.

There are few human remains at the Ness. So far. But we know that they were intelligent and highly creative people; sophisticated, spiritual, gregarious and competitive. In physical terms, they were much like us, although with a shorter life-span. Their origins were probably as mixed as ours: descendants of Mesolithic people who colonised Scotland by travelling along the coasts; folk who came to the archipelago at the start of the Neolithic,

and others who continued to flow in and out from then on.

The Ness was occupied for over a millennium and what it meant to people across that time may well have changed. But it is significant that the site lay at the heart of a remarkable complex of Neolithic funerary and ceremonial monuments. Back then, the Brodgar peninsula drew people in from near and far, to honour the dead and to celebrate important events with feasts, to renew

◄ **A SENSE OF BEAUTY** Aesthetics are specific to our time and we should not impose them on the past. But these objects are beautiful to our eyes and understanding. The question is: what did they see? What values did they place on the appearance of things and the stories they held?

◀ PEOPLE LIKE US
The people who built the Ness were people like us in all that it means to be human, but many details are missing. For now we cannot tell the colour of their eyes, their hair or even their skin. No matter. They are our ancestors, wherever we come from.

old ties and forge new bonds. When the broader world came together, many things were possible: the settling of feuds, competitions for renown, the exchange of goods, gifts and no doubt, gossip. And all of this woven around key moments of ceremony, through a sense of the spiritual that could be traced in the land and in the sky. Set apart by walls and water, the Ness was the hub around which proceedings turned, an *axis mundi* for the people of the Neolithic. We do not know how far folk travelled to attend important ceremonies. But this was a time when ideas, materials and people circulated over great distances, when stories were carried across the water and around the hearths of scattered communities. What happened at the heart of things, what was said and done, was fundamental to how people thought of themselves and their place in the world. They have gone but the stones speak for them.

THE BIG QUESTIONS

The Ness lay at the heart of an important ceremonial landscape. That much can be said with confidence, but what else can be sifted from the detritus of 5,000 years? Here are some of the big questions we hope to answer...

Time and history are pressing concerns. How long was the Ness in use? Excavation is a slow process and to dig quickly is to risk missing or damaging vital evidence, but the very beginning of the Ness is still a mystery. The oldest date thus far is 3200 BC but there are older buildings under the ones now visible and we certainly haven't reached the bottom. The other end of the scale is just as puzzling. Radiocarbon dating suggests that the Ness went out of use in 2300 BC, but what happened then? There were big changes in society, for pottery changed radically as did treatment of the dead, but how and when did this happen and did events at the Ness have any part to play?

What kind of society did the Ness serve? Was it egalitarian, with everyone more or less equal, or are there signs of a hierarchy of secular or priestly leaders? Our best guess at the moment is that a bit of both applied, but the question is still there and far from settled.

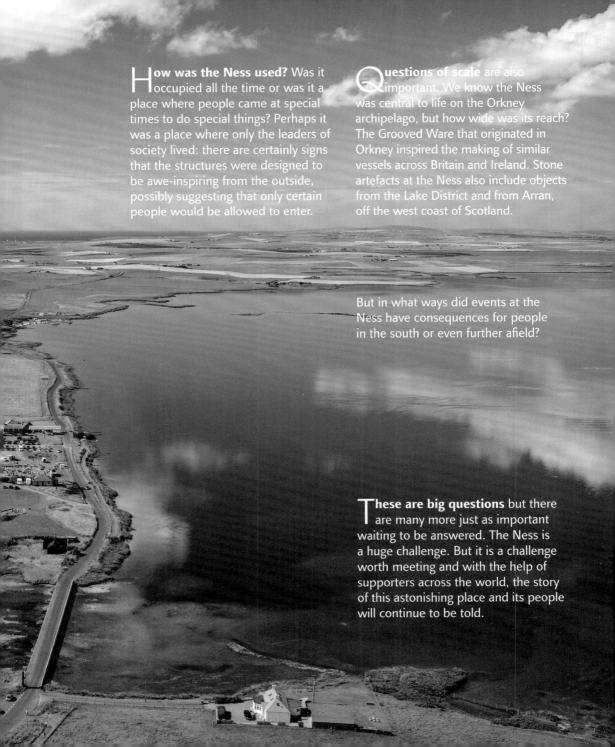

How was the Ness used? Was it occupied all the time or was it a place where people came at special times to do special things? Perhaps it was a place where only the leaders of society lived: there are certainly signs that the structures were designed to be awe-inspiring from the outside, possibly suggesting that only certain people would be allowed to enter.

Questions of scale are also important. We know the Ness was central to life on the Orkney archipelago, but how wide was its reach? The Grooved Ware that originated in Orkney inspired the making of similar vessels across Britain and Ireland. Stone artefacts at the Ness also include objects from the Lake District and from Arran, off the west coast of Scotland.

But in what ways did events at the Ness have consequences for people in the south or even further afield?

These are big questions but there are many more just as important waiting to be answered. The Ness is a huge challenge. But it is a challenge worth meeting and with the help of supporters across the world, the story of this astonishing place and its people will continue to be told.

With thanks to all the people who have helped produce this guide and everyone who has put so much effort and support into bringing the Ness of Brodgar story this far.

Words **Roy Towers**, **Nick Card** and **Mark Edmonds**
Editorial concept and design **Jo Bourne**
Editorial management **Anne Mitchell**
Editorial co-ordination **Martha Johnson**
Digital colour and prepress **Guy Sawtell**

First published in Great Britain in June 2015

ISBN 978-0-9932757-0-8

Printed and bound by Orkney Media Group Ltd,
Hatston, Kirkwall, Orkney KW15 1GJ

This guide was funded by the American Friends of the Ness of Brodgar Inc, a registered United States tax-exempt 501(c)(3) charity

PICTURE CREDITS

FRONT COVER main Jim Richardson; bottom left ORCA, bottom centre and right Hugo Anderson Whymark, **IFC-1** main Hugo Anderson-Whymark, Kenji Hattori; **2-3** top row Jim Richardson, Jo Bourne, Jim Richardson, Jim Richardson; centre row Jo Bourne, Aaron Watson, Will MacNeil, Jo Bourne; **4-5** top row Hugo Anderson-Whymark x2, Adam Stanford x3, bottom left Hugo Anderson-Whymark, bottom right ORCA; **6-7** all ORCA except panel Jo Bourne; **8-9** maps ORCA, all pictures Jim Richardson; **10-11** Top left, bottom left ORCA, top right Jim Richardson, bottom right Nicki MacRae; **12-13** all ORCA except 12 bottom centre Adam Stanford, 13 bottom left Jim Richardson and artwork Cecily Webster; **14-15** top left, bottom left and bottom right ORCA, centre left, top right, centre right Hugo Anderson-Whymark, bottom centre Jo Bourne; **16-17** all Antonia Thomas except 17 top right Jo Bourne; **18-19** top left Hugo Anderson-Whymark, top right Jo Bourne, bottom row ORCA, Jo Bourne, ORCA; **20-21** centre left, bottom left, bottom centre, ORCA, top right Hugo Anderson-Whymark, panel top left ORCA, bottom left and top right Jo Bourne, bottom right Jim Richardson; **22-23** top left Antonia Thomas, centre and bottom left ORCA, bottom centre Peter Brigham, top right Hugo Anderson-Whymark, bottom right row ORCA, Jim Richardson, ORCA; **24-25** all ORCA except centre Hugo Anderson-Whymark, **26-27** top left Hugo Anderson-Whymark, bottom left ORCA, top right Hugo Anderson-Whymark, bottom Aaron Watson; **28-29** main Jo Bourne, left row Aaron Watson, Michael Sharpe, Hugo Anderson-Whymark, right row Natasha Bourne; **30-31** Jim Richardson; **32-IBC** left to right Jim Richardson x2, Hugo Anderson-Whymark, Jim Richardson, Hugo Anderson-Whymark, Jim Richardson, Hugo Anderson-Whymark, Jo Bourne x2; **BACK COVER** Jim Richardson